TITUBA

By WILLIAM MILLER

Illustrated by
LEONARD JENKINS

Gulliver Books • Harcourt, Inc. • San Diego • New York • London

www.harcourt.com

Gulliver Books is a registered trademark of Harcourt, Inc.

Library of Congress Cataloging-in-Publication Data
Miller, William, 1959–
Tituba/by William Miller; illustrated by Leonard Jenkins.—1st ed.
p. cm.
"Gulliver Books."
Summary: Story of Tituba, a West Indian slave who was unjustly accused of witchcraft
at the outset of the Salem, Massachusetts, witch trials.
1. Tituba. 2. Witches—Massachusetts—Biography—Juvenile literature.
3. Witchcraft—Massachusetts—Juvenile literature. 4. Slaves—Massachusetts—Biography—
Juvenile literature. 5. Trials (Witchcraft)—Massachusetts—Salem—Juvenile literature.
[1. Tituba. 2. Witchcraft—Massachusetts. 3. Slaves—Massachusetts. 4. Trials (Witchcraft)—
Massachusetts. 5. Women—Biography.] I. Jenkins, Leonard, ill. II. Title.
BF1575.M55   2000
974.4'5—dc21
[B]   99-6332
ISBN 0-15-201897-2

First edition

H G F E D C B A

Printed in Singapore

*The illustrations in this book were done in spray paint, acrylics, and pastels
on museum board.*
The display type was set in Opti Packard Bold.
The type was set in Cheltenham Book.
Printed and bound by Tien Wah Press, Singapore
This book was printed on totally chlorine-free Nymolla Matte Art paper.
Production supervision by Pascha Gerlinger.
Designed by Leonard Jenkins and Judythe Sieck

AUTHOR'S NOTE

Tituba was a slave accused of witchcraft during the Salem witch trials in 1692. She came to New England from Barbados in the West Indies after she was bought by the Reverend Samuel Parris. In New England she cared for the Reverend Parris's daughter and niece and entertained them with stories of Barbados—stories about talking animals and the magic practiced on her native island, including fortune-telling. When the two young girls began to act strangely—crying out and barking like dogs—Tituba was accused of witchcraft, as were several other women. Tituba confessed to the crime, presumably in order to save her own life. Nineteen people who did not confess were executed. Tituba herself spent thirteen months in a Boston jail until she was exonerated and bought by a new slave master. Nothing else is known about Tituba after her release from jail. This book is a creative attempt to tell her story and fill in the missing periods of her life.

TITUBA LOVED THE MORNING LIGHT. The rising sun flooded the valley, turning the banyan leaves and palm fronds to burning gold.

When she went to fetch water, the mice and macaws spoke to her. "Good morning, mistress," they said.

"And to you," she replied.

When Tituba's jar was filled to the brim, she thanked the water spirits.

In the evenings Tituba sat in her doorway,
telling fortunes.

"Throw the shells," the men and women
pleaded. Tituba shook the seashells in both
hands, then threw the shells across a bright
cloth she had woven. Tituba answered questions
by reading the patterns the shells made.

"A storm is coming," she said to the men who watched over the crops. "You will marry before the next harvest," she told an anxious girl.

One night Tituba asked the shells what the future held for her. "This cannot be!" she exclaimed. She threw them again only to see the same terrible vision.

Tituba had been a slave all her life, and the next day, when she was working in the cane field, her master, Mr. Parris, appeared. Mr. Parris told Tituba and a few of the other slaves that they would soon travel with him to a far-off land, a place called Boston.

Tituba did not want to leave the island—it was the only home she had ever known—but she had no choice.

A week later Tituba found herself in the
hold of a ship. The motion of the waves made
her sick; the darkness wrapped her like a frozen

shawl. Would she ever see the sun again? She
and the other slaves huddled together. They
had never felt so frightened or alone.

The ship rocked across the sea more days and nights than Tituba could count, until at last it reached its destination.

The city of Boston was crowded with carts and shouting men; the air smelled of fish and black smoke. Tituba took care of her master's daughter and his niece, mending their clothes, preparing their meals. She was used to hard work, but she missed the island, the sunlight, the trees, the birds that had greeted her every morning.

One morning Mr. Parris announced that the family was moving to Salem Village. Tituba dressed the girls while the oxcarts were loaded. *At least we are going to a village,* she thought. *At least we are leaving the city behind.*

Their new house was on the edge of a stony field. It was small and dark, but once more Tituba breathed fresh air and heard the songs of birds as they flew from tree to tree.

One cold night just after the master had left the house, Tituba was alone with his daughter and niece. They were no longer little children, but young girls full of questions.

"Tell us about the sea," Elizabeth, the younger of the two, asked.

"Tell us about the island," Abigail joined in.

Tituba told them about the water spirits, and the mice and parrots that called to her on the way to the stream.

That night the two girls had strange dreams.
Elizabeth dreamed of Tituba's homeland, of flying
over the blue mountains, and a green, endless

sea. Abigail dreamed of talking birds and mice,
and a strange cat with red eyes that called her
by name.

The next night the girls asked again about Tituba's life in her homeland. She told them she could read fortunes by the patterns shells made when thrown on a special cloth.

"Tell ours! Tell ours!" both shouted at once. Tituba did as they asked but was frightened by what she saw. She told them that nothing but good fortune was ahead, then quickly sent them to bed.

In the weeks that followed, the girls had stranger and stranger dreams. They dreamed that women from the village came into their room at night, pricking their feet with pins, calling out the name of the devil.

When they told their father about the dreams, he became frightened. "Only a witch could cause such dreams," he declared. "The elders must be told at once!"

Tituba was brought before the court, accused of witchcraft. Other women stood beside her in the dock—the very women the girls had dreamed about.

"Are you a witch?" the judge asked Tituba. She wanted to defend herself, to tell the court that she had only told the girls about her ancient island beliefs. But who in this room of accusing eyes would believe her?

"I am not a witch," she said quietly.

Like Tituba, the other women denied that they were guilty of anything. They begged the court to let them go home.

Suddenly Elizabeth and Abigail fell to the floor, writhing like snakes. "Witches, witches—all of them, witches!"

Tituba was thrown into a dark cell with the other women, told to confess to the crime of witchcraft or be put to death.

As the days passed, the jail filled with even more women accused of the same crime.

In the cell, dark as the hold of a slave ship, Tituba turned her eyes to the wall. There was no prison worse than the fear she felt now. Loneliness lay down beside her.

Once more Tituba was brought before the court. The eyes of the whole village were on her: She recognized the elders, their wives, the young girls who had caused so much pain. Her master stared at her with cold angry eyes.

"Confess or die," the judge demanded.

Tituba longed to defend herself, to tell the court that she came from another land with beliefs different than their own. *I have only spoken of my island—what I learned*

from those who came before me, she thought. *How could it be wrong to speak of these things?*

"Confess or die," the judge said again.

Tituba looked down at the stone floor, knowing that she must save her own life. "I confess," she said with a trembling voice.

Again the young girls squealed and writhed, demanding that all the women confess. . . .

The terror lasted for many months. Some who refused to confess were put to death. Then, as suddenly as it had begun, the terror ended. The women who had confessed were set free when their families paid for their time in jail. Soon Tituba was alone.

One night in her cell, Tituba prayed for death to come. "Let me suffer no more!" she cried out to the spirits.

She waited, but death did not come. Instead the moon rose above the frozen fields, shone its pure light between the bars of her cell. It was the same moon that shone on the green sea, flooding the valleys of her island with a light that turned night into day.

A smile, the first in months, spread across her face. "Thank you," she whispered to the moon.

The jailer woke her the next morning before dawn. "Your master has sold you—he wants to be rid of you once and for all."

Tituba was sent to work in another household, far from Salem Village. She kept to herself and found peace when the sun shone brightly and the trees were in full bloom.

Sometimes she thought about escaping, running toward the woods for any freedom she could find. But how far could she really go? How long before she would be returned and punished?

One spring her master bought five young slaves from the island on which she was born. She saw herself in their eyes—alone, frightened, sick for home.

They looked to Tituba for help.

In the evenings she threw the shells and told their fortunes. "One day, freedom will come. A master might own your body, but he can never own your spirit," she told them. "Remember where you're from. Remember the banyan trees and birds that speak. Remember what your fathers and mothers told you about the spirit world."

"Look up at the sky," she told them. "The same moon and stars shine on everyone, slave or free. And who can ever own the sky?"